50 Best Mac and Cheese Dishes

By: Kelly Johnson

Table of Contents

- Classic Baked Mac and Cheese
- Stovetop Mac and Cheese
- Lobster Mac and Cheese
- Bacon Mac and Cheese
- Buffalo Chicken Mac and Cheese
- Jalapeño Popper Mac and Cheese
- Truffle Mac and Cheese
- Pulled Pork Mac and Cheese
- BBQ Mac and Cheese
- Four-Cheese Mac and Cheese
- Garlic Parmesan Mac and Cheese
- Chili Mac and Cheese
- Smoked Gouda Mac and Cheese
- Creamy White Cheddar Mac and Cheese
- Philly Cheesesteak Mac and Cheese
- Shrimp Mac and Cheese
- Broccoli Mac and Cheese

- Sausage Mac and Cheese
- Pepper Jack Mac and Cheese
- Vegan Mac and Cheese
- Mac and Cheese with Breadcrumb Topping
- Southern Baked Mac and Cheese
- Cauliflower Mac and Cheese
- Mac and Cheese Stuffed Peppers
- Caramelized Onion Mac and Cheese
- Spinach and Artichoke Mac and Cheese
- Cheeseburger Mac and Cheese
- Butternut Squash Mac and Cheese
- Crab Mac and Cheese
- BBQ Brisket Mac and Cheese
- Pesto Mac and Cheese
- Mac and Cheese Muffins
- Greek Mac and Cheese with Feta
- Kimchi Mac and Cheese
- Ranch Chicken Mac and Cheese
- Roasted Garlic Mac and Cheese

- Hot Honey Mac and Cheese
- Fried Mac and Cheese Balls
- Tater Tot Mac and Cheese Casserole
- Cajun Mac and Cheese
- Mushroom and Swiss Mac and Cheese
- Breakfast Mac and Cheese with Egg
- Beer Cheese Mac and Cheese
- Sun-Dried Tomato Mac and Cheese
- Blue Cheese Mac and Cheese
- Meatball Mac and Cheese
- Mac and Cheese Waffles
- Alfredo Mac and Cheese
- Tex-Mex Mac and Cheese
- Baked Ziti Mac and Cheese

Classic Baked Mac and Cheese

Ingredients:

- 8 oz elbow macaroni
- 2 tbsp butter
- 2 tbsp flour
- 2 cups milk
- 2 cups shredded cheddar cheese
- Salt and pepper to taste
- 1/2 cup breadcrumbs (optional, for topping)

Instructions:

1. Preheat oven to 375°F. Cook pasta until al dente; drain.
2. In a saucepan, melt butter, whisk in flour to make a roux.
3. Gradually whisk in milk and cook until thickened.
4. Stir in cheese, salt, and pepper until melted.
5. Combine with pasta and pour into a baking dish.
6. Top with breadcrumbs if desired and bake for 20–25 minutes.

Stovetop Mac and Cheese

Ingredients:

- 8 oz pasta
- 2 tbsp butter
- 1 cup milk
- 1 ½ cups shredded cheddar cheese
- Salt and pepper

Instructions:

1. Cook pasta and drain.
2. In the same pot, melt butter, stir in milk, and bring to a simmer.
3. Add cheese and stir until melted.
4. Add pasta back in and stir to coat. Serve immediately.

Lobster Mac and Cheese

Ingredients:

- 8 oz pasta
- 2 tbsp butter
- 2 tbsp flour
- 2 cups milk
- 1 cup shredded gruyère
- 1 cup shredded cheddar
- 1 cup cooked lobster meat, chopped
- Paprika and parsley for garnish

Instructions:

1. Prepare cheese sauce with roux and milk, then stir in cheeses until smooth.
2. Add lobster and cooked pasta, mix well.
3. Bake at 375°F for 20 minutes or serve hot stovetop-style.

Bacon Mac and Cheese

Ingredients:

- 8 oz pasta
- 6 slices bacon, cooked and crumbled
- 2 tbsp butter
- 2 tbsp flour
- 2 cups milk
- 2 cups shredded cheddar cheese

Instructions:

1. Make cheese sauce as usual, then stir in crumbled bacon.
2. Mix with cooked pasta and bake or serve hot.

Buffalo Chicken Mac and Cheese

Ingredients:

- 8 oz pasta
- 1 cup cooked shredded chicken
- 1/3 cup buffalo sauce
- 2 tbsp butter
- 2 cups milk
- 2 cups cheddar cheese
- Optional: blue cheese crumbles

Instructions:

1. Stir buffalo sauce and chicken into cheese sauce.
2. Mix with pasta and top with blue cheese if desired.
3. Bake at 375°F for 20 minutes or serve warm.

Jalapeño Popper Mac and Cheese

Ingredients:

- 8 oz pasta

- 2 tbsp butter

- 2 tbsp flour

- 2 cups milk

- 1 ½ cups cheddar cheese

- 1/2 cup cream cheese

- 2 fresh jalapeños, diced (or pickled)

- Optional: crumbled bacon

Instructions:

1. Prepare cheese sauce with cheddar and cream cheese.

2. Stir in jalapeños (and bacon if using), then mix with pasta.

3. Bake or serve immediately.

Truffle Mac and Cheese

Ingredients:

- 8 oz pasta
- 2 tbsp butter
- 2 tbsp flour
- 2 cups milk
- 1 ½ cups gruyère or white cheddar
- 1 tbsp truffle oil

Instructions:

1. Make cheese sauce and stir in truffle oil.
2. Combine with pasta and bake for 20 minutes or serve hot.

Pulled Pork Mac and Cheese

Ingredients:

- 8 oz pasta
- 2 cups shredded pulled pork
- 2 tbsp butter
- 2 tbsp flour
- 2 cups milk
- 2 cups cheddar cheese
- Optional: BBQ sauce drizzle

Instructions:

1. Mix cheese sauce with pulled pork and cooked pasta.
2. Bake at 375°F for 20 minutes, drizzle BBQ sauce on top before serving.

BBQ Mac and Cheese

Ingredients:

- 8 oz pasta
- 1 cup chopped BBQ meat (chicken, brisket, etc.)
- 1/3 cup BBQ sauce
- Cheese sauce: butter, flour, milk, cheddar

Instructions:

1. Stir BBQ sauce and meat into cheese sauce.
2. Mix with pasta and serve or bake for 20 minutes at 375°F.

Four-Cheese Mac and Cheese

Ingredients:

- 8 oz pasta
- 2 cups milk
- 1/2 cup each: cheddar, mozzarella, parmesan, and gouda
- 2 tbsp butter
- 2 tbsp flour

Instructions:

1. Create roux with butter and flour, then whisk in milk.
2. Add all cheeses and melt until smooth.
3. Mix with pasta and bake for 25 minutes at 375°F.

Garlic Parmesan Mac and Cheese

Ingredients:

- 8 oz pasta
- 2 tbsp butter
- 2 tbsp flour
- 2 cups milk
- 1 ½ cups shredded parmesan cheese
- 4 cloves garlic, minced
- Salt and pepper

Instructions:

1. Melt butter in a saucepan, add garlic, and sauté until fragrant (about 1 minute).
2. Stir in flour to make a roux, then gradually whisk in milk.
3. Once thickened, stir in parmesan and mix with pasta.
4. Season with salt and pepper. Serve immediately.

Chili Mac and Cheese

Ingredients:

- 8 oz pasta
- 1 cup chili (homemade or canned)
- 2 tbsp butter
- 2 tbsp flour
- 2 cups milk
- 2 cups shredded cheddar cheese
- 1 tsp cumin (optional)
- 1 tsp chili powder

Instructions:

1. Prepare chili and set aside.
2. Make cheese sauce with butter, flour, milk, and cheese.
3. Mix in chili, season with cumin and chili powder.
4. Combine with pasta and serve hot.

Smoked Gouda Mac and Cheese

Ingredients:

- 8 oz pasta
- 2 tbsp butter
- 2 tbsp flour
- 2 cups milk
- 1 cup shredded smoked gouda cheese
- 1 cup shredded sharp cheddar cheese
- Salt and pepper

Instructions:

1. Make cheese sauce by melting butter, adding flour, and whisking in milk.
2. Stir in gouda and cheddar until melted.
3. Combine with cooked pasta, season with salt and pepper, and serve.

Creamy White Cheddar Mac and Cheese

Ingredients:

- 8 oz pasta
- 2 tbsp butter
- 2 tbsp flour
- 2 cups milk
- 2 cups shredded white cheddar cheese
- Salt and pepper

Instructions:

1. Prepare a roux with butter and flour.
2. Gradually whisk in milk to make a creamy base.
3. Stir in white cheddar cheese until smooth.
4. Mix with pasta and season with salt and pepper to taste. Serve hot.

Philly Cheesesteak Mac and Cheese

Ingredients:

- 8 oz pasta
- 1 lb thinly sliced beef steak (e.g., ribeye)
- 1 bell pepper, chopped
- 1 onion, sliced
- 2 tbsp butter
- 2 tbsp flour
- 2 cups milk
- 2 cups provolone cheese
- Salt, pepper, and garlic powder

Instructions:

1. Cook steak, peppers, and onions in butter until tender.
2. Make a cheese sauce by melting butter, adding flour, and whisking in milk.
3. Stir in provolone cheese until melted.
4. Mix in steak and veggie mixture with cooked pasta.
5. Season with salt, pepper, and garlic powder, then serve.

Shrimp Mac and Cheese

Ingredients:

- 8 oz pasta
- 1 lb shrimp, peeled and deveined
- 2 tbsp butter
- 2 tbsp flour
- 2 cups milk
- 2 cups shredded cheddar cheese
- 1 tsp paprika
- Salt and pepper

Instructions:

1. Sauté shrimp in butter with paprika, salt, and pepper until cooked. Set aside.
2. Prepare cheese sauce with butter, flour, milk, and cheddar.
3. Stir in shrimp and combine with cooked pasta.
4. Serve immediately.

Broccoli Mac and Cheese

Ingredients:

- 8 oz pasta
- 2 cups broccoli florets, steamed
- 2 tbsp butter
- 2 tbsp flour
- 2 cups milk
- 2 cups shredded cheddar cheese
- Salt and pepper

Instructions:

1. Steam broccoli until tender.
2. Make a cheese sauce with butter, flour, milk, and cheddar.
3. Stir in steamed broccoli and cooked pasta.
4. Season with salt and pepper. Serve hot.

Sausage Mac and Cheese

Ingredients:

- 8 oz pasta
- 1 lb sausage (Italian, breakfast, or your choice)
- 2 tbsp butter
- 2 tbsp flour
- 2 cups milk
- 2 cups shredded cheddar cheese
- Salt and pepper

Instructions:

1. Cook sausage in a skillet, breaking it into crumbles.
2. Prepare cheese sauce with butter, flour, milk, and cheddar.
3. Mix sausage into the cheese sauce and combine with pasta.
4. Season with salt and pepper and serve hot.

Pepper Jack Mac and Cheese

Ingredients:

- 8 oz pasta
- 2 tbsp butter
- 2 tbsp flour
- 2 cups milk
- 1 cup shredded pepper jack cheese
- 1 cup shredded cheddar cheese
- Salt, pepper, and cayenne pepper (optional for extra heat)

Instructions:

1. Prepare a cheese sauce with butter, flour, and milk.
2. Stir in pepper jack and cheddar cheeses until smooth.
3. Season with salt, pepper, and cayenne (if using).
4. Mix with cooked pasta and serve hot.

Vegan Mac and Cheese

Ingredients:

- 8 oz pasta
- 1 cup raw cashews (soaked in water for 2 hours)
- 1/4 cup nutritional yeast
- 1/2 cup unsweetened almond milk
- 1 tbsp lemon juice
- 1 tsp garlic powder
- 1/2 tsp turmeric (for color)
- Salt and pepper

Instructions:

1. Drain soaked cashews and blend them with almond milk, nutritional yeast, lemon juice, garlic powder, turmeric, salt, and pepper until smooth.
2. Heat the sauce in a saucepan over medium heat, stirring occasionally.
3. Combine with cooked pasta and serve.

Mac and Cheese with Breadcrumb Topping

Ingredients:

- 8 oz pasta
- 2 tbsp butter
- 2 tbsp flour
- 2 cups milk
- 2 cups shredded cheddar cheese
- Salt and pepper
- 1/2 cup breadcrumbs (preferably panko)
- 1 tbsp butter (for the breadcrumb topping)

Instructions:

1. Prepare mac and cheese sauce by making a roux with butter, flour, and milk, then stirring in cheese.
2. Mix with cooked pasta.
3. Melt 1 tbsp butter in a skillet, then toast breadcrumbs until golden.
4. Pour mac and cheese into a baking dish, top with toasted breadcrumbs, and bake at 375°F for 10–15 minutes until bubbly and golden.

Southern Baked Mac and Cheese

Ingredients:

- 8 oz elbow macaroni
- 2 tbsp butter
- 2 tbsp flour
- 2 cups whole milk
- 2 cups shredded sharp cheddar cheese
- 1 cup shredded mozzarella cheese
- 1/2 cup heavy cream
- 1/4 tsp garlic powder
- 1/4 tsp onion powder
- Salt and pepper to taste
- 1/2 cup crushed Ritz crackers (for topping)

Instructions:

1. Cook macaroni and drain.
2. Prepare a cheese sauce with butter, flour, milk, heavy cream, garlic powder, onion powder, and shredded cheeses.
3. Mix pasta with cheese sauce and transfer to a greased baking dish.
4. Top with crushed crackers and bake at 350°F for 20–25 minutes until golden and bubbly.

Cauliflower Mac and Cheese

Ingredients:

- 8 oz pasta
- 1 small cauliflower head, cut into florets
- 2 tbsp butter
- 2 tbsp flour
- 2 cups milk
- 1 ½ cups shredded cheddar cheese
- Salt and pepper

Instructions:

1. Steam cauliflower florets until soft, then blend with 1 cup of milk until smooth.
2. Make a cheese sauce with butter, flour, and the remaining milk.
3. Stir in blended cauliflower and cheddar cheese, seasoning with salt and pepper.
4. Combine with cooked pasta and serve.

Mac and Cheese Stuffed Peppers

Ingredients:

- 4 large bell peppers
- 8 oz pasta
- 2 tbsp butter
- 2 tbsp flour
- 2 cups milk
- 2 cups shredded cheddar cheese
- Salt and pepper

Instructions:

1. Cut tops off bell peppers and remove seeds.
2. Cook pasta and prepare mac and cheese sauce with butter, flour, milk, and cheese.
3. Stuff peppers with mac and cheese, then bake at 375°F for 20–25 minutes until peppers are tender.

Caramelized Onion Mac and Cheese

Ingredients:

- 8 oz pasta
- 2 large onions, thinly sliced
- 2 tbsp butter
- 2 tbsp flour
- 2 cups milk
- 2 cups shredded cheddar cheese
- Salt and pepper

Instructions:

1. Caramelize onions by cooking them slowly in butter until golden and soft.
2. Prepare cheese sauce with butter, flour, and milk.
3. Stir in caramelized onions and cheddar cheese.
4. Combine with cooked pasta and serve.

Spinach and Artichoke Mac and Cheese

Ingredients:

- 8 oz pasta
- 2 tbsp butter
- 2 tbsp flour
- 2 cups milk
- 1 cup shredded parmesan cheese
- 1 cup shredded mozzarella cheese
- 1/2 cup frozen spinach, thawed and drained
- 1/2 cup canned artichoke hearts, chopped
- Salt and pepper

Instructions:

1. Prepare cheese sauce with butter, flour, milk, and cheeses.
2. Stir in spinach and artichokes.
3. Combine with cooked pasta and serve.

Cheeseburger Mac and Cheese

Ingredients:

- 8 oz pasta
- 1 lb ground beef
- 1 tbsp ketchup
- 1 tbsp mustard
- 2 tbsp butter
- 2 tbsp flour
- 2 cups milk
- 2 cups shredded cheddar cheese
- Salt and pepper

Instructions:

1. Cook ground beef, seasoning with salt and pepper. Stir in ketchup and mustard.
2. Make cheese sauce with butter, flour, milk, and cheddar.
3. Mix beef with sauce and combine with pasta. Serve hot.

Butternut Squash Mac and Cheese

Ingredients:

- 8 oz pasta
- 2 cups roasted butternut squash, pureed
- 2 tbsp butter
- 2 tbsp flour
- 2 cups milk
- 2 cups shredded cheddar cheese
- Salt and pepper

Instructions:

1. Roast butternut squash until soft, then puree.
2. Make cheese sauce with butter, flour, milk, and cheese.
3. Stir in pureed squash and combine with pasta.
4. Serve warm.

Crab Mac and Cheese

Ingredients:

- 8 oz pasta
- 1 lb crab meat (fresh or canned)
- 2 tbsp butter
- 2 tbsp flour
- 2 cups milk
- 2 cups shredded cheddar cheese
- 1/2 tsp Old Bay seasoning
- Salt and pepper

Instructions:

1. Cook pasta and set aside.
2. Make cheese sauce with butter, flour, milk, and cheddar cheese.
3. Stir in Old Bay seasoning, crab meat, salt, and pepper.
4. Combine with pasta and serve hot.

BBQ Brisket Mac and Cheese

Ingredients:

- 8 oz pasta
- 1 lb BBQ brisket (shredded)
- 2 tbsp butter
- 2 tbsp flour
- 2 cups milk
- 2 cups shredded cheddar cheese
- 1 tbsp BBQ sauce
- Salt and pepper

Instructions:

1. Shred cooked brisket and set aside.
2. Prepare cheese sauce with butter, flour, milk, and cheddar.
3. Stir in BBQ sauce, brisket, and seasoning.
4. Combine with cooked pasta and serve immediately.

Pesto Mac and Cheese

Ingredients:

- 8 oz pasta
- 1/4 cup pesto (store-bought or homemade)
- 2 tbsp butter
- 2 tbsp flour
- 2 cups milk
- 2 cups shredded mozzarella cheese
- 1/2 cup grated parmesan cheese
- Salt and pepper

Instructions:

1. Cook pasta and set aside.
2. Make cheese sauce with butter, flour, milk, mozzarella, and parmesan.
3. Stir in pesto and mix with pasta.
4. Serve hot with extra parmesan if desired.

Mac and Cheese Muffins

Ingredients:

- 8 oz pasta
- 2 tbsp butter
- 2 tbsp flour
- 2 cups milk
- 2 cups shredded cheddar cheese
- 1/4 cup breadcrumbs (for topping)
- Salt and pepper
- 1/4 cup grated parmesan cheese

Instructions:

1. Prepare mac and cheese sauce with butter, flour, milk, and cheese.
2. Mix with cooked pasta and spoon into greased muffin tin.
3. Top with breadcrumbs and parmesan.
4. Bake at 350°F for 15–20 minutes until golden and bubbly.

Greek Mac and Cheese with Feta

Ingredients:

- 8 oz pasta
- 2 tbsp butter
- 2 tbsp flour
- 2 cups milk
- 1 ½ cups shredded mozzarella cheese
- 1/2 cup crumbled feta cheese
- 1/4 cup chopped Kalamata olives
- 1/4 cup diced cucumber (optional)
- Salt, pepper, and dried oregano

Instructions:

1. Prepare cheese sauce with butter, flour, milk, mozzarella, and feta.
2. Stir in olives, cucumber, oregano, salt, and pepper.
3. Combine with cooked pasta and serve.

Kimchi Mac and Cheese

Ingredients:

- 8 oz pasta
- 1 cup kimchi, chopped
- 2 tbsp butter
- 2 tbsp flour
- 2 cups milk
- 2 cups shredded cheddar cheese
- 1 tbsp gochujang (Korean chili paste)
- Salt and pepper

Instructions:

1. Cook pasta and set aside.
2. Sauté kimchi in butter for 2–3 minutes.
3. Make cheese sauce with butter, flour, milk, cheddar, and gochujang.
4. Stir in kimchi, mix with pasta, and serve hot.

Ranch Chicken Mac and Cheese

Ingredients:

- 8 oz pasta
- 1 lb cooked chicken, shredded
- 2 tbsp butter
- 2 tbsp flour
- 2 cups milk
- 2 cups shredded cheddar cheese
- 1/4 cup ranch dressing
- Salt and pepper

Instructions:

1. Cook pasta and set aside.
2. Shred cooked chicken.
3. Prepare cheese sauce with butter, flour, milk, cheddar, and ranch dressing.
4. Stir in shredded chicken, season with salt and pepper.
5. Mix with pasta and serve.

Roasted Garlic Mac and Cheese

Ingredients:

- 8 oz pasta
- 1 head garlic, roasted
- 2 tbsp butter
- 2 tbsp flour
- 2 cups milk
- 2 cups shredded cheddar cheese
- 1/2 tsp thyme (optional)
- Salt and pepper

Instructions:

1. Roast garlic by wrapping it in foil and baking at 400°F for 30–40 minutes.
2. Squeeze roasted garlic out and mash it.
3. Prepare cheese sauce with butter, flour, milk, cheddar, and mashed garlic.
4. Season with thyme, salt, and pepper.
5. Mix with pasta and serve hot.

Hot Honey Mac and Cheese

Ingredients:

- 8 oz pasta
- 2 tbsp butter
- 2 tbsp flour
- 2 cups milk
- 2 cups shredded sharp cheddar cheese
- 1 tbsp hot honey (or mix honey with chili flakes)
- Salt and pepper
- Red pepper flakes for extra heat

Instructions:

1. Prepare cheese sauce with butter, flour, milk, and cheddar cheese.
2. Stir in hot honey and season with salt, pepper, and red pepper flakes for extra spice.
3. Mix with cooked pasta and serve hot.

Fried Mac and Cheese Balls

Ingredients:

- 8 oz pasta
- 2 tbsp butter
- 2 tbsp flour
- 2 cups milk
- 2 cups shredded cheddar cheese
- 1/4 cup grated parmesan cheese
- 1 egg, beaten
- 1 cup breadcrumbs
- Vegetable oil for frying

Instructions:

1. Prepare mac and cheese as usual, making a cheese sauce and mixing with cooked pasta.
2. Let the mac and cheese cool and set in the fridge for at least an hour.
3. Roll the mac and cheese into small balls.
4. Dip each ball into beaten egg, then coat with breadcrumbs.
5. Heat oil in a deep fryer or large pan and fry the balls until golden and crispy.
6. Serve with marinara sauce or ranch for dipping.

Tater Tot Mac and Cheese Casserole

Ingredients:

- 8 oz pasta
- 2 tbsp butter
- 2 tbsp flour
- 2 cups milk
- 2 cups shredded cheddar cheese
- 1 bag frozen tater tots
- Salt and pepper
- 1/2 tsp garlic powder

Instructions:

1. Prepare cheese sauce with butter, flour, milk, and cheddar cheese.
2. Mix with cooked pasta and season with salt, pepper, and garlic powder.
3. Transfer pasta mixture to a baking dish.
4. Top with frozen tater tots and bake at 375°F for 20–25 minutes, until tater tots are golden and crispy.

Cajun Mac and Cheese

Ingredients:

- 8 oz pasta
- 2 tbsp butter
- 2 tbsp flour
- 2 cups milk
- 2 cups shredded cheddar cheese
- 1 tbsp Cajun seasoning
- 1/2 tsp paprika
- 1/2 tsp garlic powder
- Salt and pepper
- 1/2 lb cooked shrimp (optional)

Instructions:

1. Prepare cheese sauce with butter, flour, milk, and cheddar cheese.
2. Stir in Cajun seasoning, paprika, garlic powder, salt, and pepper.
3. If desired, mix in cooked shrimp.
4. Combine with pasta and serve hot.

Mushroom and Swiss Mac and Cheese

Ingredients:

- 8 oz pasta
- 1 cup mushrooms, sliced
- 2 tbsp butter
- 2 tbsp flour
- 2 cups milk
- 2 cups shredded Swiss cheese
- Salt and pepper
- 1/4 tsp thyme (optional)

Instructions:

1. Sauté mushrooms in butter until tender and golden.
2. Prepare cheese sauce with butter, flour, milk, and Swiss cheese.
3. Stir in sautéed mushrooms, thyme, salt, and pepper.
4. Combine with pasta and serve hot.

Breakfast Mac and Cheese with Egg

Ingredients:

- 8 oz pasta
- 2 tbsp butter
- 2 tbsp flour
- 2 cups milk
- 2 cups shredded cheddar cheese
- 1/2 tsp garlic powder
- Salt and pepper
- 2 eggs (scrambled)
- 1/4 cup cooked bacon or sausage (optional)

Instructions:

1. Prepare cheese sauce with butter, flour, milk, cheddar, garlic powder, salt, and pepper.
2. Scramble the eggs in a pan and cook until just set.
3. Mix the scrambled eggs and cooked bacon or sausage (if using) into the cheese sauce.
4. Combine with cooked pasta and serve warm.

Beer Cheese Mac and Cheese

Ingredients:

- 8 oz pasta
- 2 tbsp butter
- 2 tbsp flour
- 1 cup milk
- 1 cup beer (lager or pale ale)
- 2 cups shredded sharp cheddar cheese
- 1/4 cup grated parmesan cheese
- Salt and pepper

Instructions:

1. Prepare cheese sauce with butter, flour, milk, beer, cheddar, and parmesan.
2. Season with salt and pepper to taste.
3. Mix with cooked pasta and serve immediately for a rich, tangy twist.

Sun-Dried Tomato Mac and Cheese

Ingredients:

- 8 oz pasta
- 2 tbsp butter
- 2 tbsp flour
- 2 cups milk
- 2 cups shredded mozzarella cheese
- 1/4 cup chopped sun-dried tomatoes (packed in oil)
- Salt and pepper
- Fresh basil for garnish

Instructions:

1. Prepare cheese sauce with butter, flour, milk, and mozzarella.
2. Stir in sun-dried tomatoes, salt, and pepper.
3. Combine with cooked pasta and serve garnished with fresh basil.

Blue Cheese Mac and Cheese

Ingredients:

- 8 oz pasta
- 2 tbsp butter
- 2 tbsp flour
- 2 cups milk
- 1 cup shredded cheddar cheese
- 1/2 cup crumbled blue cheese
- Salt and pepper

Instructions:

1. Prepare cheese sauce with butter, flour, milk, cheddar, and blue cheese.
2. Season with salt and pepper to taste.
3. Combine with cooked pasta and serve hot for a creamy, tangy mac and cheese.

Meatball Mac and Cheese

Ingredients:

- 8 oz pasta
- 1 lb ground beef or turkey
- 1/4 cup breadcrumbs
- 1/4 cup grated parmesan cheese
- 1 egg
- 2 tbsp olive oil
- 2 tbsp butter
- 2 tbsp flour
- 2 cups milk
- 2 cups shredded mozzarella cheese
- Salt and pepper
- 1 tsp garlic powder

Instructions:

1. Make meatballs by mixing ground meat, breadcrumbs, parmesan, egg, salt, and pepper. Shape into small balls.
2. Brown meatballs in olive oil over medium heat. Set aside.
3. Prepare cheese sauce with butter, flour, milk, and mozzarella.
4. Combine the cooked pasta, meatballs, and cheese sauce.

5. Serve hot, garnished with extra parmesan and parsley.

Mac and Cheese Waffles

Ingredients:

- 8 oz pasta
- 2 tbsp butter
- 2 tbsp flour
- 2 cups milk
- 2 cups shredded cheddar cheese
- 1/4 cup grated parmesan cheese
- 1 egg
- 1/2 cup breadcrumbs
- Salt and pepper

Instructions:

1. Prepare cheese sauce with butter, flour, milk, cheddar, and parmesan.
2. Mix cheese sauce with cooked pasta.
3. Add egg to pasta mixture, then spoon it into a preheated waffle iron.
4. Cook until golden and crispy.
5. Serve with extra cheese or a drizzle of hot honey for extra flavor.

Alfredo Mac and Cheese

Ingredients:

- 8 oz pasta
- 2 tbsp butter
- 2 cloves garlic, minced
- 2 cups heavy cream
- 2 cups shredded mozzarella cheese
- 1/2 cup grated parmesan cheese
- Salt and pepper
- Fresh parsley (optional)

Instructions:

1. Cook pasta and set aside.
2. In a pan, melt butter and sauté garlic until fragrant.
3. Add heavy cream and bring to a simmer.
4. Stir in mozzarella and parmesan, and season with salt and pepper.
5. Combine the cheese sauce with the pasta and serve garnished with parsley.

Tex-Mex Mac and Cheese

Ingredients:

- 8 oz pasta
- 1 tbsp olive oil
- 1/2 lb ground beef or turkey
- 1 packet taco seasoning
- 2 tbsp butter
- 2 tbsp flour
- 2 cups milk
- 2 cups shredded cheddar cheese
- 1/2 cup diced tomatoes with green chilies
- 1/4 cup chopped cilantro
- Jalapeño slices (optional)

Instructions:

1. Brown the ground meat in olive oil, then stir in taco seasoning and set aside.
2. Prepare cheese sauce with butter, flour, milk, and cheddar cheese.
3. Stir in diced tomatoes with green chilies and the cooked meat mixture.
4. Combine with cooked pasta and top with cilantro and jalapeños for an extra kick.

Baked Ziti Mac and Cheese

Ingredients:

- 8 oz pasta (ziti or elbow)
- 2 tbsp butter
- 2 tbsp flour
- 2 cups milk
- 2 cups shredded mozzarella cheese
- 1/2 cup grated parmesan cheese
- 1 cup marinara sauce
- 1/2 tsp garlic powder
- Salt and pepper
- 1/2 cup breadcrumbs

Instructions:

1. Cook pasta and set aside.
2. Prepare cheese sauce with butter, flour, milk, mozzarella, and parmesan.
3. Mix the cheese sauce with pasta, then stir in marinara sauce.
4. Transfer to a baking dish, top with breadcrumbs, and bake at 375°F for 20 minutes until golden and bubbly.

www.ingramcontent.com/pod-product-compliance
Lightning Source LLC
LaVergne TN
LVHW081323060526
838201LV00055B/2434